GASTROMYTHOLOGY

POEMS

JESSICA MANACK

Sheila-Na-Gig Editions

Gastromythology ©2024 Jessica Manack

Cover image: Jessica Manack, collage

Author photo: Michael Cuccaro

ISBN: 978-1-962405-49-2

Sheila-Na-Gig Editions
Russell, KY
Hayley Mitchell Haugen, Editor
www.sheilanagigblog.com

ACKNOWLEDGMENTS

The author is grateful to the editors of the publications in which some of these works previously appeared:

Birthing: "Breastfeeding at Forty," "Core Competency"
Black Fork Review: "Dad Visits Me at College"
Five South: "Where"
High Shelf Press: "Transubstantiation"
If and Only If: "Perilous Figures"
Impost: "Bath in the Tears of Rachel Carson"
Maintenant: "The House I Built Didn't Have a Roof Until I Shouted Your Name"
Maudlin House: "The Guts of '80s Kids"
Northern Appalachia Review: "Office Ladies"
Orca, a Literary Journal: "Gastromythology," "In the Mothers' Room"
Peregrine: "The Smallest Town in Maryland"
Prime Number Magazine: "The Call of the Campervan"
Sheila-Na-Gig online: "Cornucopia"
SLAB: "Sweet Quantifications"
Untelling: "The Right to Ruin"
Wild Roof Journal: "Preparations"
Women Speak: "Archaeology," "Highway Lifecycle," "Miracle Season," "The Ring Bearers"

These poems would not exist without the communities that have helped me keep the pen moving, even when life has tried to pull me away. To those at Hollins University, Lit Youngstown, the Appalachian Writers Workshop, the Women of Appalachia Project, and Pen Parentis, I remain grateful for your warm embrace.

Thank you to those who have provided careful reading and feedback on many of these poems: Cathryn Hankla, Jenn Blair, William Woolfitt, Jack Christian, Michele Summerlin Grace, Matthew Lippman, Marianne Worthington, and Jana-Lee Germaine.

To Ralph and Cora: Always write down your stories.

To Michael: Thank you for your love and support, which has made this all possible.

CONTENTS

Archaeology

We may as well have been Columbus, da Gama,
my brother and I, born into a world they called New:
pastless, plastic, no photos on the walls, only
tchotchkes on the mantels, only our fairy tales.
We lived in a suburb sprung up around the airport,
history-free, formerly farms.

We played outside in those days, banished
to the kids' kingdom, so Mom could have her Stories,
Days, One Life to Live, sharing a play-by-play
with her sister over the phone. Other people's stories.
Our shadowy corners were something to
peroxide, to hide, create antidotes against.

We made potions, mixed berries and petals.
The hydrangeas bloomed their aluminum blue.
We dug in the dirt in our yard, one day
unearthing trash 1940s fires had failed to burn,
small glass vials, metal toothpaste tubes.
We learned that people here had been wilder,

only recently imposing the suburban order.
In metal barrels the trash burned out back,
secrets vanishing quicker than S'mores.
We spread out our evidence, asking questions.
Who had been here before? Why had they left?
What brought us here? What kept us here?

We didn't know our mother didn't even know
her grandmother was alive, confined to an asylum.
We didn't know our grandmother's teenage
pregnancy was the reason her family moved
three states away one summer, sudden East-coasters.
We only knew stories burbled under the surface,

noses poking up through the seafoam.
Baby detectives, we were unquenchable,
skeptical, magnifying-glassed, leaving no junk
drawer unemptied, finding what there was to find.
We scratched and scrabbled and scoured,
asking only, if we hadn't been meant to know,
would we have been fitted with these little claws?

I

The Ring Bearers

for Joseph Hall, 1845-1908

Joseph strode deep into the woods.
He did every day—raised in them, rich from them—
but this day was different, with Alice gone,

gone forever, yet still there, at rest in the front room.
She had just learned to walk, but the fever
bested her, put her to sleep forever.

And he knew that the other children needed to see
his strength, his faith, even when he could not
be sure of it himself. So it was only in front of

the hemlocks that he wailed, the trees breathing in
his exhalations, his carbon dioxide, to use for sugars,
to add mass, the sum of all that year's inputs.

The rings buried deep trapped his grief
to hold it forever, the cries locked inside
1886, 1887, 1888 when he lost his babies

to typhoid: first Alice, then Hattie, and Bessie,
all gone before the age of three. How wrong
that these unloving monoliths should endure.

But they did, and grew fat on the weeping.
And with the trees Joseph fed his family,
felling the elders to send down the rivers,

down the Clarion, the Ohio, the Mississippi, towns
and houses springing up as quickly as the wood came,
made sturdy from the names of the lost.

What Kind of Woman

for Harriet Huling Hall, 1845-1913

My third great-grandmother was born in 1845
and yet I have many pictures of her face,
looking in each like a president, someone on money,
frozen and feelingless, maybe a caryatid, holding

the weight of the world on her head.
In each picture, she sits, stern, bearing
the fixed features necessary for the camera,
hoping her face will last the ages.

It was hard to know how she really felt—
happy, healthy, suffering from a toothache?
Glad to age beside her husband?
Mourning the babies lost to the plague?

Her clear eyes were constants, her fine dress,
a neat bun of dark hair, eventually spectacles,
the cloud of children surrounding her
moving too quickly to capture.

But she lived long enough to see progress:
until 1913. Around the turn of the century,
her daughter Cora got a Brownie camera,
and the snapshots followed, the scrapbooks,

the belief that their days were worth recording.
And I finally got to see what kind of woman she was—
my great, great, great grandmother.
Here, half a Harriet, blurry, laughing in the back

of a carriage bumping up a rough road,
old bones still up for a tumble.
How wicked to capture these vernaculars,
to have a way to do such things, to finally

have the means to spend so far beyond needs.
Here, graying and grinning on the farm,
staying useful until the end of her days,
the penciled caption: *collecting chips.*

Did she realize that it was in this moment
that she gave me what I needed to know?
May I never forget that I am of the stuff
that laughs when what life brings is shit.

The Smallest Town in Maryland

Port Tobacco was long exhausted, no more Tobacco,
no Port, just a sleepy cove off the Potomac. The grandmothers

and mothers were tired, too, filled their children's
pockets full of money, hoped it was enough to buy an

afternoon of peace, whichever way they fled, by land or
water, enough peace to polish off a bottle, maybe even a day

or two or three, sleeping in their week-old beehives, maybe
leaving some keys for them to find, hoping they'd pile into a car

and head to the next town, maybe over to Pope's Creek, to the
crab shack, busy for a while with a bushel, the children scavengers

like their dinner, the crabs just like the mothers, trapped
and forced to be food. And the crabs never learned, it happened

over and over, the skittering into the traps, the falling into the pots,
the bodies breached to release the meat, as easy to end as to create

life, the mothers walking that line until breathing their last, turned
by rage into ash and thrown into the river. No notice posted.

Who ever read the news? The papers lined the tables,
buffers between the Old Bay and the heirlooms, protecting

the relics while the children learned, maybe they'd finally
learn, there was no dinner without someone's broken back.

The Right to Ruin

We'd visit great-grandmother in Jacobs Creek, pass the plates of
pickled eggs and creamed cucumbers, squirrel stew,
making eyes with our mother, blinking out in code,
How much do we need to eat?

This was a victory: they used to eat lard sandwiches,
were glad to fill a belly with anything, back when
my great-grandfather wrenched a living from the ground,
lump by lump dug from the Banning mine, from the Darr mine.

My grandfather was spared the underworld, but did his own
hard labor: helping lay the railroad tracks passing his house, to carry
coal away, carry him away. Turned out he could sell anyone anything.
Now there was a spread, only nothing we were used to eating,

and no one taught us to appreciate, only annihilate:
place pennies on train tracks to see them transformed,
to know the force, a better lesson than any lecture.
The uncles would try to impress, not content with pennies,

boasting, always trying to top each other, lining up
beer cans, daring each other to use quarters, half-dollars.
Scrabbling through the rocks for Kennedy's mangled face,
they once again bloodied their knuckles in search of a glimmer.

The tracks our grandpa laid stayed firm,
steady and silent as he was, carrying people away
so they didn't have to descend into the bowels of the earth
and could return so rich there was copper to squander—

line it up and watch it be brutally smoothed.
Great-grandma always went inside by then,
leaving the porch swing shaking its disapproval.
She never needed to see how hard they'd

wreck themselves to get back at the land.
Nothing makes you feel as rich as having money to waste,
showing the land how far we'd come, how far
these rails would keep taking us from where we'd begun.

The Guts of '80s Kids

Our Tanged intestines sparkle. We survived,
guts Gonzo Graped and Purplesaurus Rexed.
No one had heard of Yellow Number 5.
Our mothers always tried to do their best.

But, Man-O-Mangoberry! I dyed my hair
with Kool-Aid once. It took a year to fade—
Rock-a-dile Red, the stubbornest flare,
a sunset more perfect than any any god made.

So now they gleam, our innards perma-rainbowed:
the Great Blue-dini spleen, heart Sharkleberry.
Our kidneys blush a darling Pink Swimmingo,
nothing Kansas-bland, no lime, no cherry;

they are my buried treasure, hidden wealth.
A bright inside for an outside beige and pasty.
We were not only feeding, but preserving ourselves—
our wrinkles like Fruit Wrinkles, ageless and tasty.

Perilous Figures

Girls are finally reclaiming mathematics,
let us rejoice, doing columns of sums
for fun, tallying, multiplying, leaving boys
in the dust, calorie counters of the world unite!
Girls are doing it right now, those smoking motors,
showing us how to run on spit and fire, on zeroes,
showing us what sort of empires the silent form.
Auto-makers, engineers, take heed:
these geniuses of consumption show us
how to go-go-go on nothing at all, how to maximize
miles per gallon, minimizing everything else.
At once girls are saints and hurricanes:
performing miracles, feeding two thousand
with one loaf, turning disgust to combustion,
moving steadily, messes of blurry lines and aerobic activity.
Deeming their silhouettes happy accidents,
not carefully crafted works of art and violence,
girls brandish their bodies at the world
as though there is nothing obscene
in having swords for collarbones,
as though there is nothing hostile
in sharpening the knives of their ribs.
Girls cannot exist outside of façade,
claiming that they already ate, that they're
late, that they're too busy to eat, too full
already of appointments and spite.
Girls lie to the world that lies to them first,
whispering: *here is an allotment to do with*
as you wish, belonging only to you,
no one wrangling it from your hands,
appraising it with lust you don't understand,
sullying it without your consent.
Girls relish the last laugh, they know what goes,
what's chaff; they know what they're doing,
how near sunlight can get to bone.

Girls know how to pare. Girls know when to stop, how to find the statue hidden under all that stone.

Bath in the Tears of Rachel Carson

Pittsburgh is rich with rivers we don't know how to love,
names taken from the people we vanquished,

the Allegheny and Monongahela braiding
to form the sparkling Ohio. But don't get too close:

shit flows regularly into the waterways,
yours, ours, theirs, a murky stew of effluvia.

I try to keep mine out, skip flushing,
let the dishes sit, save the laundry for another day,

when the sky grays and the system's burdened,
the water treatment plant unable to keep up.

Still, it's better than the old system, the lack of system,
waste flowing unimpeded into the rivers until 1959.

When it rains, when the parking-lot snow mountains melt,
the drains can't cope with the overflow, everyone knows.

But nobody cares: the trash tells the secret of how little
most ponder what's downwind. If you walk the riverside,

you'll see the muddy grey banks interrupted by rainbow.
Not the oily sheen of gasoline, but a stream of discard—

tampon applicators, the fluorescent swords that let women avoid
touching their own bodies. You could mistake them for flowers,

this wreckage left on the shores: pinks, purples and greens
so far beyond nature they sparkle even in December,

little garden blooming through the winter.
America is rich with daughters we don't know how to love

and our shame flows downstream. We arm them
with the wrong things. Mirrors and scales. Tweezers and razors.

We teach them to ruin the world they inherit, so it feels familiar,
so busy battling themselves they miss what's coming around the bend.

Miracle Season

The first one was the tights I managed not to snag.
The second, the hairspray that held me together,
taming my brittle, bleached hair: nearly respectable. Except
the lip gloss was too brash, too orangey: my grandmother

was right, though I never admitted it until today,
and it clashed with my braces, rubberbanded red and green.
Getting ready by my mother's makeup mirror set to Evening,
I hadn't yet figured out whether I was a summer or a winter.

Seasons? The only linen we ever wore was White Linen,
Mom spraying liberally enough to cover us all,
even, usually, the fumes surrounding our father.
And that was the next miracle: he'd abstained that night,

no shampoo bottle of whiskey in his waistband.
The ballet called for more, our very best behavior,
a chance for the clumsy to witness perfection.
Perhaps we'd see the dolls and mimic them;

perhaps a flame of grace would be lit within.
Since no one had recently died or married,
since our uncle's cancer had vanished
and we no longer needed to go to church,

we'd had to buy new dress clothes, always
cheap, infrequently used, too soon outgrown.
Oh, we were rich with mysteries we couldn't explain,
gangly but still glimmering, too old now to smile

on command, too old, even, for a smile to be beaten out of us.
But smile we did, in unison, still learning our best features,
trying to make our gawky faces make sense,
hoping the veneer would hold for a night, and, miracle

of miracles, it did, but we didn't get greedy, knew
it wasn't worth asking for more, watched our fate
played out on the stage: in some lives,
one night of magic was all you got.

Dad Visits Me at College

He drove the ten hours straight
  passed out on the air mattress
    in the social room

His pants were ripped
  down the ass crack
      with nothing underneath

Was he fucking with us
  or just fucked up?

He wanted to take us to dinner
  so my roommate came along, the promise of food
    or comedy too great to ignore

We all ate steaks at Applebee's
    extra onion rings
  I talked about William Cullen Bryant,
    recited lines from "Thanatopsis"

And he said, *No use being afraid to die*
  we're all gonna shit ourselves
      one of these days

I hid all the gay stuff
  ripped the pictures of Françoise Hardy
    from the walls

Walked around undercover,
  all jumpy, waiting
to be admonished for something or other
  my wet hair, the muddy cuffs
    of my jeans

And then there it was:
Honey, You should have told me
   this was
      a dry town

II

Cornucopia

The nuns taught us that there were three kinds of kisses:
peaches, prunes, and alfalfa. I said, *I don't get it,*
and you whispered: *Say it out loud.*

And I did, slowly, and blushed:
Peaches, pruuunes, al-fal-fa,
my mouth moving in ways it hadn't moved before.

They wanted us to know the enemy.
They wanted us to fear kisses the way we feared food,
wanted us to find purity through hunger,

and it was true: we were terrified.
But we already knew we weren't pure,
not after the men had had their grabs,

the ones on the bus, the sidewalk, the sneaky ones, the bold ones.
We embraced, sitting frozen for an hour, unsure what else to do,
ruined by movies, the pressure of theater.

We listened to the beating of our dark hearts,
had tried to cut the dark parts out of us,
so we nursed each other's wounds and tasted fruit—

the peaches, the prunes, blueberry, elderberry,
the dragon fruit, the kiwi, lime, lychee, the lemons,
the clementines, plums, tomatillos, our tongues delighted, acrobatic.

Done with hunger, tired of denial, we thundered upon each other
and I never thought to ask: *how would they know?* Just trusted
the sisters, that they knew we were doomed.

Until I asked: *What would happen if I told her?*
If I weren't scared of my hunger? What if I let myself be full?
And we ate and it was good.

Where

There, in the library. Free to the people. In the field outside the chapel. In the chapel. At the pulpit, whatever they call it. These places other people built for other people: we made them ours. Outside the cemetery, where no one complained. Outside the stable, where no one was disgusted. On the city bus, anonymous. In the parts of my body I had just learned to cover up. There, hungover, over eggs. Our houses might as well have been façades. We broke out at dusk, broke into song on the sidewalk. *No, we're all out of snacks! No, you can't use the bathroom!* I was named after an actress. You were named after a flower. And there, in the underpass that's always flooded, we joined our puzzle-piece teeth. We ignored the graffiti. There, on the Greyhound bus, I braved New England to find you. In the listening room, you played me Phil Ochs for the first time, dropped the needle like a professional. *There, but for fortune.* The death heavy in his voice. We chose life over and over. We chose to sink into each other.

That Kind of Night

It was the kind of night when I plopped down on the curb
and threw up on my shoes. It was the kind of light that made
everything seem like a movie set. The kind of town where
you navigated by the Cathedral. No one knew what "suburb"
meant—it was that kind of country. Theirs was the kind of shade
that never claimed to cool. Theirs was the kind of antique air

that tasted centuries old. It was the kind of wine that did you in.
They were the kind of people who appraised us with their eyes.
You were the kind of drunk whose friends refused to walk
on the same side of the street. I claimed you and your stupid grin.
You were the kind of towhead American who couldn't disguise
yourself. I was that kind of American too. I shouldn't talk.

It was the kind of fun that was desperate, an oblivion.
Ours were the kind of thirsting mouths that never said no.
These were the kind of nights with blurry ends. The kind of gay
bars that were hard to find and called "Don't Tell Anyone."
You were the kind of guy whose motto was "Let's go."
I was the kind of girl who never paused with her "OK."

Preparations

They say it's gonna be a big one, I gasp
at Neil on the long trudge up the hill to my place,
sherpa, burdened with toilet roll and cereal.
Neil sits on his porch with a Yuengling, the bottle
the only thing green as far as the eye can see.
Yep. Neil answers back, almost all there is to say.
Stocked up. Liquid bread, he laughs,
raising it in salute. It is not until then
that I wonder if all the things I have done to prepare
were the wrong things,
all the sustenance I hoarded the wrong sustenance.
I wonder if, on the second or third day,
hair matting, the cold suppressing my scent,
I will feel up to wandering out to scavenge,
wonder what I will bring myself to do to acquire
what other people smartly thought to procure,
wielding a shovel, chipping a path through the ice.
And will it be worth it, that taste of tart wheat,
sharp and sweet on the tongue?

Transubstantiation

You filled me in the way you were allowed:
a bowl of steaming curry, double-forked.
We'd cancel all our meetings for the day
and I'd ride in your car, gaily bedorked,

a blur, so fast no one could trace our steps,
to the strip mall with the Thai place no one liked.
And neither of us touched a single phone.
And neither of us thought about your wife.

We laughed and laughed, our best stories unfurled,
and snuck back to our desks two hours late.
My eyes would gleam, embarrassed with delight.
My cheeks were pinked with Spicy Level 8,

my crevices prepped, smooth and jasmine-ripe,
in case this was the day things took a turn.
You never touched me and I don't know why.
Was there a lesson I had failed to learn?

Were you as scared as I to take a step?
Or keeping me a dangling backup plan?
Why had I confused you for a god,
you spiceless, frightened noodle of a man?

The House I Built Didn't Have a Roof
Until I Shouted Your Name

How small's the sound of colossal things breaking: a rattling. A rug
shaken out. Snow falling like bone dust. Pulverized cloud. Cheeky
bones, lazy bones, funny bones: gone hollow. Blanched marrow.

I had memorized each of your parts, could have filed them in plastic
pouches like the archaeologist whisking her soft brush over femurs
and teeth. Each piece in its place, and no room for nostalgia. But for
you, pursuit was the pleasure, possession passé.

When *you* die, you'd reminded me, you want to be made into plates.
Bone china. Nobody will dig you up in 2,000 years, speculate, measure
hips, count teeth. Embarrassing, that would be, to be so scrutinized,
like seeing the gynecologist at the grocery.

Awkward, like talking to the grizzled man two houses down, the man
who whittles and, if asked why, says, "Some things are more beautiful
broken," the secret of bone-setters, of geodes, of the spines of books.

Saffron

You seemed a sandwich (ham), easy to love (not tricky
to devour), familiar with a little zip: clump of mustard,
lip of swiss. Or peanut butter, maybe—something rib-sticky,
hearty, thick. Yes, the heaves and the jiggles of custard,
bread heady with yeast, crust yielding to sweet porous meat,
made me think of you. As did steaming spaghetti:
a puzzle, a mass to unravel, a source of joy and heat.
Put another way: I thought you'd sustain me.

But dear, you've failed me so; what aliment is this?
I eat five times a day, by rote, am never filled,
for you are merely chicken broth, the tang of boiled stone,
brackish and translucent; flavor's gravestone, vigor's piss.
Yes, you are instant saffron rice: starchy vaguely brill-
iant, and yellow, yellow, yellow: yellow-bellied, yellow-boned.

Gastromythology

The day after you leave, I realize that I am starving, and that I am in the place for it. Stopping at each stand on the street, I buy cones of almonds saltier than the sea, steal enough hazelnut paste to last a week, hide bananas like disease up my shirtsleeves. I cry in cafeterias, clean cups with my tongue, trying each tea—Black Forest, Dreams of Rilke—without luck. None of these are what my mouth wants to be full of. I'm displaced: a flopping fish, dismembered hand, in a land where words lay like traps in the way. The people here greet friends with *Hey, Uncle.* They say: *I have the head of three in the afternoon* and *Your girlfriend is gorgeous; she is like a train.* The last time you went away was the day I learned the vigor of cheese, all kinds. The sly, pillow-softs, the ink-blue clots, the ones with waxy rinds: I made them mine, storing in oil for next time what I didn't eat. Now, I hang out beside the bakery, drinking yogurt, grinding fried corn between my teeth, until fresh bread drops down the chute into the window. I eat it as I walk. It lasts a block. At the candy stand by my house, the old man studies me as though I am a lush, tired eyes pink as Valentines. "For the kids," I lie. You're always on the go. You don't send notes, or cards, or steaks at Christmastime. I try to gild goodbyes, frost them pink and sweet like cakes, but I can't hide my eyes. I seek you in every pie. I eat the promises you break with ham on rye. Flailing, I try to write you, but "You're so shellfish!" is all I manage. I eat my dinners in bars, anonymous. It feels safe. Tonight, the rotund widow brings plate after plate—fried bread soup, cauliflower drowned in mayonnaise, eggs splayed atop mountains of squash and rice, a plateful of red tuna packed in oil, veins black, an ore. Hefting her rolls while fetching me more, ignorant of my binges, she encourages me to *eat.* "The eyes of the fat are brilliant," she laughs. "The eyes of the thin, they pop out like frozen fish." The light falling away's all that punctuates my days. My feeding's never complete. I pry orange blossoms from the trees lining the streets, shower my mouth with flowers tasty as phone books. Nothing is as filling as it looks. Even the fruits on the trees are useless, used by junkies, they say, to sterilize needles—a few acidic pricks to safety. I roll one in my hand, marvel at its slick citrus skin, teeth mossy, hands soiled and clammed. It doesn't let on, but I know we're both damned, we're both shoved, bodies tested and bruised, flesh shot through with poison mistaken for love.

III

Office Ladies

A is for Audrey, who sniffles all day.
B is for Barb, who negotiated her pay.
C is for Cindy, the de facto nurse.
D is for Dot, with the flask in her purse.
E is for Eunice, who eats at her desk.
F is for Francie, who dances burlesque.
G is for Gudrun, imported to last.
H is for Holly (legendarily fast).
I is for Iris and the florals she'd waft.
J is for Jami, impeccably coiffed.
K is for Kelly, perpetually cold.
L is for Lauren, not young and not old.
M is for Mae, who is power-adjacent.
N is for Nina, who's sadly complacent.
O is for Ondine, who sneaks naps in her car.
P is for Paula, the one who'll go far.
Q is for Quinn (for sure somebody's kid).
R is for Rhonda's lost Tupperware lid.
S is for Sally of the unsilenced phone.
T is for Tate, always good for a loan.
U is for Ursula's hidden magazines.
V for Veronica with her Lean Cuisines.
W for Winnie of the stairwell walks.
X is for Xenia, who watches the clock.
Y is for Yolanda and her poker face.
Z is for Zelda, who'll inherit the place.

The Dead Mall

I guess this is heaven. Repurposed, LEED-certified. We are the
aftermath, here in our cubicles. Functionaries trading freedom for
dollars. We don our shiny collars. Appreciate the view of the
highway. Calculate the severity of our evening commute. Enjoy the
stream of coal cars, the climate control. Coffee's brought in, food's
brought in. There's no hard-won Orange Julius costing an hour's
wage, after taxes. No ups, no downs, no furtive kisses behind the
wayfinding signage. No soft pretzel bought with the promise of a
later favor. No walking, perfectly coiffed, down the corridor, past the
sum of the town. No hushpuppies. Oh, hush, puppy, at least it
wasn't razed. At least we can bring our kids to stare and say, here is
where it all used to happen. A website is no place for a heartquake.
You want to be somewhere where you can walk in a circle that never
stops. Where behind every storefront is a smiling Denise, a glam
Tammy, ready to sell you something to take the pain away.

The Man From the Bluebird Club

gives a lunchtime presentation
over chicken salad sandwiches.

His topic: the preservation of the habitat
of the eastern bluebird, a protected species.

Our employer gives us a break from our
cubicles to show their support of wildlife.

If we can make a place for nesting, maybe
everyone will forget about the chemicals.

Outside our window, the accountants play
cornhole, tallying and bellowing.

The man explains that the house sparrow
is not from here, but introduced and invasive.

They displace the native bluebirds,
prevent them from thriving. He explains

how to catch them in a burlap sack, snap
their necks, ensure quick deaths. Do our part.

I went to this talk because I love birds, not
because I feel capable of murdering them.

I want to say: come, sparrows, I'll feed you, native
or not, I know about thriving without belonging.

Breastfeeding at Forty

It might be sour, what I have to give,
this drink too full of all I can't unknow.
Though you no longer need my heat to live,
you hold me down and make the time go slow.

Time, what is time? How rich I used to be—
the hours that I spent on girlish arts!
I taste of time, a wise old rind of cheese,
made tender by the beatings of my heart.

You help, though gravity needs none from you,
to pull my flesh more quickly to the earth.
Your grandmother, I'm frequently assumed;
I try to see my wealth and not my dearth.

It's easiest to let the mammal win,
to put one life away, the next begin.

In the Mothers' Room

The milk comes, drop after drop in line, an army of nourishment.

The milk comes without being asked, in words. When it can't yet be summoned with words.

The milk comes to the chatter of a pump—*backhoe, backhoe, backhoe*—steady as a clock, plinking into bottles like I'm sweating pennies, like I'm full of money.

The milk comes even when I hate myself. Through rain and snow and heat and gloom of night. She gets the best of me. She gets the worst of me.

The milk comes and some days it's the only thing I do well. The milk comes and some days it's the only time I sit still. The milk comes even when I'm not sitting still, carrying the baby as I check on her brother, careful to not disengage her.

I undo a lifetime of being taught that some things should be covered up, try to stifle the siren by giving her what she wants.

And the milk comes, mostly from Righty. (Lefty's a slouch.)

The milk comes, and no one understands just how *tired* being food makes you. How hungry being food makes you. The milk comes, mostly organic. Comes whether I fill my belly with kale or candy. I am a superfood. I am a super dude.

The milk comes. I'm a little factory. The milk comes and I'm a secret agent: moving food in secret, border-eschewer. Is this commerce? Should my transport be taxed?

I panic at a lack of snacks: hunter, gatherer. The milk comes and I'm simply mammal: not human, not hominid. The milk comes and I squeeze to move it along, curb the urge to moo, to chew my cud.

The milk comes in buttery fountains, in sugary showers, but it tastes like time.

The milk comes. Even when I forget to write MAKE MORE MILK on my to-do list.

The milk comes whether I remember to make it or not, soaking through my t-shirt as I sleep, souring the sheets, scoffing at my hatred of waste.

The milk comes and I am deflated, suddenly unbuxom, gone from bombshell to mom-shell.

The milk comes and the baby grows fat, too fat, an over-proofed loaf, angry skin raw inside the rolls, waiting for her to grow long instead of wide.

News of my guts, immunity-juice, the milk comes: the thread that connects us, a dinner, an honor, an armor.

My Son Says "Pom"

when he means "poem."
Not "pome" or "poe-em" or "pwim."
He says "pom"
in spite of the many times
I have said the word to him: *po-em.*
In spite of the example I've set.

He says "pom," maybe shorthand
for *pomegranate,* his favorite fruit,
something tart and sweet,
something nourishing, vitamin-rich.
Or maybe *pomme,* or *pomme de terre*—
something round, something that fills you.

Or does he mean something fuzzy,
something you'd hug, like *pomeranian?*
Or *pom-pom,* a thousand soft
impulses bound at the core?
Is it mishearing or a little rebellion,
a way for him to shape his tiny world?

Sometimes I think he must mean *palm,*
not the tree, with its shading fronds,
but a hand, open, ready to be read.
Ready to set a course for a future.
Ready to give, ready to receive,
the beauty in the exchange.

Sweet Quantifications

I want my children to glide through the world, unencumbered,
without the burden of worry over the invisible labors behind
it all. I don't need them to see me making the socks clean,
staying up late to wash them. I want *them* to run through fields,
not lament my obligation. Maybe they'd be cognizant of a small tension,
the way a head pinches a bit with the drop of barometric pressure.
When I want them to ponder the choreography that brought
us just here—the union of the wind and rain and sun and soil—

I manifest this in a tomato, hand over a ripe parcel, say:
thank the sunlight that traveled 93 million miles here,
the storm, the blossom. Thank the nameless bee, the rabbit
who got its breakfast elsewhere. Know that I toiled, but from it
came something sweet, know how many impulses per day,
how many braided fingers sing: *this is all for you, for you, for you.*

Core Competency

Every woman contains multitudes, from the moment of her birth:
millions of eggs waiting inside her. Each month, the release happens,

often without notice, the next precious cell queuing in the pinball chute.
But, as one ages, the urgency asserts itself,

the potential of fertility dwindling, number of cycles finite.
And we feel it even more acutely, the camel squeezing through the needle's eye.

Is pain even pain until we give it a German name?
Something guttural like the groans one makes on the chaise:

Mittelschmerz, middle-pain, the twinge in the core of your being,
in the center of every cycle, the insistent clock, the cranky jalopy.

The pain intensifies as does the scrutiny, as catcallers squint,
wonder if they should whistle or grimace? *Mittelschmerz*:

this pain of being in-between, neither sylph nor crone,
forced to go on making my face each day.

I gasp over the stove, feeding the babies and the grandmas,
never-rester in the center of this home and I call it *mittelschmerz*.

So many middles to be in—the cheese in a family sandwich,
the middle of an administration, mid-coup,

midwestern, surrounded on all sides, wondering if I should dig a hole down,
if that might buy me a private minute in the warm center of the earth.

In the warm center of my girth: *mittelschmerz*,
that kick in the ribs that says *It's sexytime, bitch—*

let me not forget that I wield great power.
Let me name it so that, when it's gone, there's a word for what I lost.

The Call of the Campervan

Klaus's wife was like the Sphinx, all square jaw and silence. Her English wasn't as good as his. It wasn't her choice to come over here; there was little use in pretending. But she attended the party, dutiful. There was a cake, though no one believed he'd done what he'd been sent here to do. It seemed as though there should be a cake. He talked about their itinerary, pulling maps out of his jacket pocket. First Canada, over the summer, then down through the U.S. and a while in Mexico. He now measured his life out in Whiles. He talked about the shower in the camper, its 6 square feet. He talked about the awning under which they'd have coffee, watching the rising sun. The vice presidents frowned. The accountants smiled. He'd been a good boss, had had me and my boyfriend to their place for fondue one evening, some cheese he'd snuck over in his luggage, the real deal. We laughed and laughed, full bottles of wine replacing the empties. We shared airport stories, road trip stories, stories not requiring idioms. Finally someone looked for a clock and then said, *Is it broken? It says 3:45 a.m.* In some stories this is where everything gets all wiggly, but Klaus kept it on the up and up. Nobody was drunk: all that bread. In the conference room, the cake started to sweat. We broke the fire code. He told us again about the five shirts they were each keeping. He told us about how the table turned into a bed. Oh, Klaus! Klausie-Mausie! I pinched his bicep, a thumbful of tweed, said, *You won't be needing these any more!* He said, *Every day this week I go home, take off my suit, and use it to clean the garage.*

Highway Lifecycle

The vultures have all day.
They glide above us, above the trees,
smirk at our urgency

and profit from it, as below we do
their dirty work, speed through the streets, lay waste
to nature, pile carcasses on the side of the road.

Paint stripes as if to say: here, you feast,
erase our shame so we may kill again
as you watch from above, keeping our secrets.

About the Author

Jessica Manack holds degrees from Hollins University and lives with her family in her hometown of Pittsburgh, Pennsylvania. Her writing has appeared widely in anthologies and journals, including *Still: The Journal*, *SWWIM Every Day*, and *Fine Print*, and has been nominated for a Pushcart Prize. She is a recipient of a 2022 Curious Creators Grant. This is her first book. Keep up with her work at http://www. jessicamanack.com